Daniil Dragos - PhD Nicolae I Ionescu

Europe: to be, or not to be - that is the Question!

DEDICATION

We dedicate this essay to all people who acknowledge that only "the truth is the *truth*."

Daniil Dragos

Was engineer in oil rigs manufacturing in Ploiesti. Worked for Control Data Corporation - USA, in Research and Development and later on as Market Development Manager for East Europe (computer sales and the first postwar American manufacturing joint venture in Eastern Europe). Worked in Research and Development in Automation and computers in Bucharest. Was counselor and Deputy Director in the Ministry of Foreign Trade - Bucharest (negotiations of Cernavoda Nuclear Power Plant, of cars manufacturing with Renault and Citroen - France etc.). Was Fullbright Visiting Scholar at Graduate School of Management, University of California, Los Angeles (UCLA).

PhD Nicolae I. Ionescu

PhD in world economy. Was Ambassador of Romania to Sweden. Was senior official at the United Nations, agreed by the General Secretary of the UN. Served as Chief of Section for Least Developed Countries at UNIDO - Vienna. Was director and general manager in the Ministry of Foreign Affairs of Romania. Was member of the core team for the negotiation of the Association Agreement of Romania with the European Union. Is author of a book and articles.

CONTENTS

Europe: to be, or not to be - that is the
Question   7 - 87

Motto:
"Even if you are a minority of one, the *truth* is the *truth*." *Mohandas Karamchand Gandhi*
(2 October 1869 - 30 January 1948)
"The greatest sin of men is fear, fear of looking ahead and acknowledging the truth. It is cruel, this truth, but it's the only of any use." *Mihai Eminescu,*
(27 January 1850 - 27 June 1889).

Europe: to be, or not to be - that is the Question...

The phone is ringing; annoyingly insistent. As the years go by, I enjoy less and less talking on the phone. And Rori -my wife- is not home to answer it! I pick up nervously the receiver
.-"Hullo!"
- "Yes!"
-"Are you really annoyed that a friend of yours is calling you, or let's say, just a former colleague at the Ministry of Foreign Trade?" Recognizing the voice of His Excellency the Ambassador Marin Ionescu, I was suddenly relieved.
-"My friend, my friend, the *Ambassador...*"

-"It's OK that you have not forgotten completely the English language. Can you guess why I'm calling you?"

-"Certainly! It means that you have received my email and read it."

-"Right! Besides, I wanted to let you know that I finished reading your book; from the first to the last page. I had an interesting talk with the guy who brought it to me; namely your nephew the priest - the Romanian 'popa' by profession, as you express yourself in your book. You could have brought that book personally."

-"My nephew, who had come to Bucharest from Transylvania to visit me, told me that he did not meet in all his life an ambassador. So I gave him a chance to know one."

-"I enjoyed your book, though I should have been angry with you..."

-"Why? Didn't I write exactly what you said?! I was left with the impression that the conversation was interesting, and you, according to your custom, told the 'truth, the whole truth and nothing but the truth.'.Only the truth always!"

- "Do you mean to say that in our world they can no longer live without truth, and that those who speak it are rewarded? When I read those pages, I was thinking of scolding you, to remember me for a while. Why he didn't ask for my prior consent, I thought. Or why didn't he present only my politically correct ideas in his book?! Then, I thought, why not?! It's a free country, after all! As you often repeat it in your book... After I finished reading both your book and the email, I got an idea... "

- "What do you mean?"

-"From where do you think I am calling you?"

-"From your apartment located in the center of Bucharest, Romania... Or, maybe, you have returned to Ploiesti City..."

- "You almost guessed correctly. I returned to Ploiesti, but also I remain in Bucharest. Two days ago, I received the Penthouse apartment that I bought in the most exclusive 'Primaverii' District of Bucharest. In the commercial ad I found it was said to be of absolute luxury. The other day, I signed also the purchase contract for a pub, which I want to turn it into a *bistro* like those in Paris. Do you still hear me? Or, the conversation was interrupted?..."

-"I hear you, I hear you... But my speech is gone. That much money! Did you recover your losses from your foreign currency speculations? Or have you won the big lottery prize?"

-"More than a big lottery prize. Finally, all the properties of my uncle in Ploiesti were returned to me. What, only bigwig politicians are allowed to have a rotten-rich aunt Tamara!? Am I not allowed to have a rich uncle?! Unfortunately, he died before the Revolution of December 1989."

-"What exactly did you inherit?"

-"Three vineyards with cellars in Valea Calugareasca Vineyards, a restaurant, a workshop that has become factory in Ploiesti and other properties. Find out that my uncle had no other heirs."

-"An outstanding performance! It is said that it is not easy to get such retrocessions. Are you a friend of some VIP, who through his closest friends and relatives, intervened at the National Authority for Restitution of Property?"

-"You realize that if that were the reality, I would not even recognize it for anything in the world; knowing that now they are listening the phones even more steadily than before. The real truth - to use your word - is that I am too legalistic to resort to such methods. I just took a good lawyer, I turned to Justice and I won."

-"Congratulation!"

-"Let me tell you what idea I got after reading your book and email. By the way, why is your email written in English?

-"Originally, I sent it to friends in America and Austria. Then I thought I'd send it to you and to two or three Romanian friends too. Being lazy to translate it, I used the copy-paste, leaving the text written in English."

-"Just fine! It fits nicely with what I thought. At the inauguration of my apartment, I intend to organize frank discussions on the subject of your email. So, please transmit my kind invitation to all those to whom you sent your email."

-"I see, you imagine that they will come to Bucharest, from United States and Austria, just to have the honor of attending the inauguration of your luxury apartment."

-"I hope you've found out in what day, month, and *Anno Domini* we are today... So they do not need to come to Bucharest. Those in the United States and Austria can sit comfortably at their offices or in their armchairs, joining our discussions by Skype."

-"I see that with regard to modern Information and Communication Technology, you are more up to date than myself."

-"Thank you for the compliment. OK! You will summon them. See which is the right day for everyone. You also have to take into account the time zone differences. I'll send you my new email address. Those whom I will have the honor of receiving in my apartment are asked to take into account that I'm going to try on them some of the meals and drinks from my future *bistro's* menu. The *bistro* is currently undergoing a renovation. I intend to organize, periodically, political discussions on topical issues at the *bistro*. Following the example of the *Club of Rome*. A small and informal Club, of course. Let's see what you have to say about the name I chose for my *bistro*. 'Monsieur Marin - Bistro & frank discussions.' What do you say?!"

-"Why the French '*Monsieur*'? Why don't you use Romanian words?"

-"Because *bistro* is a French typical small restaurant. The Russian word *bystro* (*быстро*), '*quickly*' was first used by the Russian cossacks and officers, during Napoleon's time and the Battle of Paris in 1814."

-"And why the English for the *frank discussions?*"

- "Because almost all Romanians speak English. Even the lady minister in the Romanian Government, who pronounced, some weeks ago, a funny speech in New York. So, what do you say about the name I chose?"

-"It's great! You have a commercial talent. I think it will be a real financial success.."

-"A friend of mine from France found me a young French man; I hired him for two years. He will cost me much more than a local guy; I want to introduce the rules and the French home-style cooking and beverages from the Paris *bistros*. He's not only a waiter but a skilled cook as well. Sorry I held you too much on the phone."

-"That's OK!. I enjoyed talking to you. I forgot to ask... Mrs. Ionescu will be present at the discussions? In that case I will have to come with proper flowers."

-"For a while, she will stay in Ploiesti. She takes care of everything we have there. She's more talented on administrative matters than me. Let us clarify another matter ... The topic we are going to debate is sensitive, we would need a proper moderator in place."

-"I can bring Professor Marius Badescu. He's an extraordinary moderator. He encourages others to participate in discussions. Unlike the vast majority of Romanian moderators who, to show how smart they are, they speak more than all the other participants together."

-"I see you speak about the one who published with you the essays and articles on economic themes. In English and Romanian... "

-"I believe that after Professor Anghel Rugina and Professor N. N. Constantinescu died, Professor Badescu remained the greatest Romanian economist alive. In particular, in macroeconomic issues. "

-"OK! I'll be happy to meet him personally."

It did not take more than a week, and in a beautiful autumn day, we showed up at the entrance door of Ambassador Marin Ionescu's luxury apartment. Together with me were Professor Badescu, Emy Flora and Adrian Portzan. Emy Flora was born in a town close to the village where I was born. With Adrian Portzan I was a high school colleague. For a long time he worked as a senior scientific researcher at a Romanian Academy's history institute, being one of the country's reputed historians.

-"What, just a few?! Exclaimed Ambassador Marin Ionescu (or my friend the Ambassador, as I say from sympathy). "We've made arrangements to prepare dinner for much more persons. Drinking will not be a problem, but the remaining food will be ruined."

-"Do not worry! I haven't eaten since the day before yesterday. So I'll eat like three hungry guys." Adrian Portzan said, smiling.

After the American fashion, Marin Ionescu presented to us in detail the whole apartment; That is, the two bathrooms, as well. In order to make him happy, we welcomed his luxurious apartment with admiration. Then we were taken to the living room. I noticed that a huge screen was placed opposite to an enormous window with drawn curtains. My friend the Ambassador put into operation the lap top, to which a projector was connected. A greeting appeared on the screen which said 'Welcome! Bon Appétit and sincere exchange of opinions!' Then he said:

-"The dinner will be served immediately. I am interested in participating in all the discussions; so the food will be prepared and served by a young Parisian who will be also the boss of the staff of my future bistro. Discussions will be moderated by Professor Badescu. In a quarter of an hour, we will be connected with the foreign participants in our discutions. According to the list of Skype addresses received from our friend Dan, in addition to those present here, Mrs. Kate Shagall, Mr. Corneliu Lahovari and Ovidiu Dragos Jr. - from the United States - and Mr. Herman Prashunder from Austria will participate in our talks. You know the subject of the discussion."

-"I would propose an addition to the announced theme." I put forth for consideration. "My kind request is that, after finishing with the main subject, we should also refer to the situation in Romania. Those present at this excellent dinner being Romanian citizens, are highly interested in what is happening to us. Given the fact that the foreign citizens, participating from abroad at these discussions, have lived and worked for years in Romania, their comments will be particularly interesting and relevant."

The only objection came from my high school colleague Adrian Portzan.

-"It would have been normal not to wait until today to ask for this addition. Just the same, let it be! But why only after the main subject?! I find that, as a rule, Romania is always and everywhere left behind. Let us have the freedom to refer to Romania and to anything else when we choose."

-"Here is a rational proposal! You are a real historian. "Emy Flora said. "Regarding the fact that everyone leaves Romania to the rear, they should know that the New Testament says:'*So the* last *shall be* first *and the first will be last*...*"(Matthew 20:16)"

-"Very good! I like that." Said Professor Badescu "But, you did not cite the sentence to the end. You forgot to add: '*for many be called, but few chosen*' The meaning of that is: '*the last will be first*' in heavens, not in this world of ours. I don't believe that "*the first will be last*"; for example, the German nation will not be the last anymore, in the next thousand years. Not even ad infinitum. Though Germany started and lost two world wars."

Exactly at fixed time, His Excellency Marin Ionescu told welcome to foreign participants and agreed with them the rules of the game in which the debates will be held. The names of the participants were also presented. Since the present

Romanians spoke English, it was agreed that everyone would speak, in English. Professor Badescu took the proper place at the table to moderate discussions.

-"Dear Madam, dear sirs, I understand that you have all received the respective email of Mr Dragos

-" My exception..."Again, problems from my colleague Adrian Portzan. "I have not received anything. Or maybe it was deleted by my wife accidentally."

- "It's nothing serious. I ask someone to read it. At least we'll better remember its content."

-"I'll do this to practice my English, which started to rust out." Told my friend the Ambassador "OK, here's the text:"

'On account of your experience and knowledge, I would like to ask you several questions. These days, all TVs are talking and talking about the refugees. And I got confused. When that happens, usually I look into a history book published by two American professors. Specifically, I read about the fall of the Roman Empire, the followings: *The barbarians... rather suddenly began to move. Sometimes they first sought peaceable acces to the Empire... desiring with a child-like eagerness to share in the advantages of Roman civilization. More often,...(they) moved swiftly and by force."* Probably, the Romans tried to assimilate (integrate) the heathen, backward and poor barbarians. They even built walls (in today Great Britain and Romania, for example). But nothing worked. *"In 476 the last Roman Emperor in the West was deposed by a barbarian chieftain."*

We know also that, centuries later, the Ottoman Turks conquered the Byzantine Empire (Constantinople fell in 1453).

It is strange, but the rich and civilized Romans and Byzantines did not succeed to assimilate the backward barbarians and the wild Ottoman Turks. It was the other way around! The barbarians and the Ottoman Turks assimilated all Romans and Byzantines. The Turks were close to conquer all Europe. Vienna was besieged by the Turks twice (in 1529 and 1683). Fortunately, they had been finally stopped. In Turkey itself, the assimilation continued until the 20th and the 21-st centuries. It is said that in 1915, under Ottoman Turks rule, took place the killing of between 800,000 to 1.5 million Armenians. Nowadays, the powerful Turkish army used artillery against the Kurdish people.

Now, here are the questions.

-Do you think that there is a similitude between the facts shown above and what happens nowadays? Or, is foolish to make such a parallel?

-Do you think that (as an example) the French will succeed to assimilate their immigrants?

On the TV, it was said that today only about 50% of the population of France is French; the other half is formed by persons from their former colonies (Asia, Africa) or by immigrants from other parts of the world. In Great Britain, an important part of the inhabitants are not English either. They say that Berlin is the second Turkish city after Istanbul. On the TV, I saw crowds of refugees in the German *Bahnhofs*. A Saxon from Transylvania, elected in *Bundestag*, said on a Romanian TV station, that Turks born in Germany can not be integrated even after 30-40 years. They say that it will be a *"demographic suicide of Europe"*. By peaceful means, not by scimitar or by force as centuries ago! The newcomers have 5 or even more children, not 1 or 2, or no children at all, like the Europeans.'

"Sorry for the wrong pronunciation of some of the words."

-"Mrs. Kate Shagall, being the only lady who participates in our discussions, rightly compels me to pray her to take the floor" Professor Badescu said..

-"Thank you, for inviting me to give my opinion on the subject matter. You do realize, though, that this would be simply the view of an ordinary citizen, not of an Washington insider."

-"Excuse me for the interruption," I said, "but I would like to introduce Mrs. Kate Shagall, in a few words. Currently, she is a retired person resident in California. She worked for 20 years in Romania as a cultural and press counselor of the US Embassy in our country and as the Director of the American Library in Bucharest. At that time, she took PhD degree in Romania. As a writer, she published a novel in English and Romanian. I have read Mrs Kate Shagall's novel, both in Romanian and in English. In my opinion, it is the best novel about Romanians and Romania, after those written by Liviu Rebreanu, Petru Dumitriu and Marin Preda. I am not a literary critic, but I am an old consumer of literature. I have read not only all the important Romanian novels, but also the classic foreign ones. The ones written by American, English and French classics, I read them in their original languages. I say all this not to praise myself, but to show that my appreciation is not without foundation."

-"I do not want to upset anyone," my colleague Adrian Portzan said smilingly, "but I find this classification a hazard. Especially because it is done by an engineer with no university studies related to fiction and literature. So I personally have doubts that my high school colleague might figure out if a novel is good or bad."

-"I have no studies regarding wine and winery neither. So, I do not know how to make a good wine. But all of that does not prevent me from realizing that this French wine which my friend the Ambassador serves us, is an excellent wine. On the label of the bottle I see that it is written: *Meursault Louis Latour -2013, Denomination d'Origine Contrôlée – DOC.* In conclusion, I believe that, even though I don't have a license in philology, reading a novel, I can tell if it is good or bad. If you ask me on what I rely on by making the above assessment, I would say that the characters of Mrs. Kate Shagall's novel are living, that is they are alive. The atmosphere and the situations are so well described that you have the impression that the author is a Romanian rather than an American lady. Even the peasants of Bucovina look as if they were from my native village. Father Ion from the Transylvanian village resembles the priest who taught me religion during the primary school. In high school, Fane, Mendl / Mihai and Carol lived like me, while I went to high school in the Transylvanian town called Oradea. My best college and high school friend was also a Jew. Perhaps all of these were due to the fact that, for years, Bukovina and Transylvania were part of the Austro-Hungarian Empire. As far as I know, Kate Shagall's novel is one of the very few written by foreign authors, whose main characters are Romanians. I read only one other such novel, written in the time of the Austro-Hungarian Empire, by the Hungarian novelist Jókai Mór and entitled *Szegény gazdagok* (*Poor Rich Men*)."

-"I did not read Mrs. Kate Shagall's novel and I could not tell my opinion on it. However, how can you put Mrs Shagall's novel above the novels of some famous Romanian writers such as Sadoveanu, Breban or Cartarescu?! The last two were nominated for the Nobel Prize! "

-"Have you read Breban's novel, written after the Revolution of December 1989? But Cartarescu's novel titled *Levant*?"

-"I did not read them. But he who asks, did he read them?"

-"Being a stubborn reader, I read Breban's novel from the first to last page, but I could not finish Cartarescu's *Levant*."

-"You're not the only one." Emy Flora smiled ironically. "From TV I learned that one of the illustrious Presidents of our country was continuously reading Cartrescu's 'Levant' for six months, without being able to finish it."

Professor Badescu put an end to our controversy in the literature, saying, "I think we should let Mrs. Kate Shagall continue."

-"I am grateful for Dan's remarks about the book and glad he enjoyed it. I enjoyed writing it and I particularly enjoyed talking to people about their experiences here, especially the older people who went through World War II. The book is out in English and Romanian in Romania. I am not primarily interested in making money in Romania. I would like people to read the book!"

Trying to be funny, I said: "That's great! In this country, those who read books don't have money to buy them, and those who have money don't read books."

After a kind hearted laughter, Ms. Kate Shagall continued. It is easy to laugh when you have your good meals with good drinks. Especially, during a dinner with nice people.

-"Regarding the current immigration… I don't think there are many historical precedents. Much of historical immigration was specifically for war and conquest, not fleeing war with the hope of finding a safe place to settle. The Armenians were forced to leave their homes, if not killed, by the Turks. And the immigrant population in France is currently about 8.8% of the total, not half."

As usual, Ms. Kate Shagall was concise on the subject, but she did not fully convince me. So, I politely tried to object by saying:

-"It seems that you are right when you say that the official *immigrant population in France is currently about 8.8% of the total, not half.* Probably, you have that percentage from the official French statistics; which certainly are right. But we have to know what the official French statistics mean by '*immigrant population*'. I traveled quite often to France for negotiations regarding manufacturing licenses with Renault and Citroen. Also I was, 3 months in Paris, for computer training with CII. I remember that once I talked to a gentleman, who was working at the reception desk of my hotel. I thought that he was Chinese: '*Quelle est votre nationalité?*', I asked him. '*Français*', he said. I asked him again: '*Quelle est votre nationalité reele?*' He answered: '*Je suis de nationalité français*' He explained that he came from Vietnam, after the French-Vietnam war. He used to be a professor at the Saigon University. Later on, I was told by a French gentleman, that by law, all French citizens are deemed to have not just French citizenship but also French nationality (including an African that came from *Cote d'Ivoire*, a native of Arabia or a Vietnamese). So, the official 91,2% of the French population of France encloses all persons with Frech citizenship, including those who have African, Asian, or Arabic origin or those who came from other parts of the world."

-"Dear colleague," says my friend Adrian Porţan," you are talking about realities that you learned about 30-40 years ago."

-"These things can be seen nowadays if you follow any of the matches of the French national football team. Some of those who compose it are no longer resembling Athos, Porthos, Aramis, D'Artagnan, Gavroche, and other French characters of the old times; now they are a mix of genuine Frenchmen with Africans, Asians, Arabs etc. If you look at the matches of the national football teams of England, Portugal and Belgium, for example, you can see the same reality. In a recent TV show, was said that at the last year's end, the percentage of genuine British persons accounts for less than 50% of London's population. The Mayor of London is a Pakistani. If you have other data, let's hear it..."

My colleague, Adrian Porþan, was content to respond with a vague smile.

-"I think it would be appropriate to hear the views of Mr. Herman Prashunder from Austria." Professor Marius Badescu said.

-"I agree with Dan's comparison of the Roman Empire to the present situation with our Europe, but I don't want to go in more details over the open Internet. Don't worry, I think, we old people will not feel the changes in our lifetime so much, but which country will be better for our children, Europe or the USA is questionable."

Hearing this, all of us stopped suddenly from our concerns over the food and drinks on the table. Those connected via Skype were silent too. The first to have something to say was Emy Flora.

-"Our friend Dan told me, that Mr. Prashunder was an excellent salesman. Now, I find out that he is also a good futurologist and he has real diplomatic talents. His foresight for the future is cautious and realistic. I really enjoyed his remark that you need to be careful what you communicate over the open Internet. That, even in the 21st century. Or, especially in the 21st century."

We all laughed again.

- "Mr. Corneliu Lahovari follows." Professor Badescu said.

-"In regard to the matter Mr. Dragos is referring to in his email, here's my humble opinion: The huge tide of refugees toward Europe cannot be perceived as an *'invasion'* comparable to what happened in ancient times. This phenomenon has its own root causes which are completely different than the military campaigns of the Romans or of the Turks/Ottomans against neighbouring countries and/or civilizations/cultures. What we are seeing today is a humanitarian crisis of historic proportions. I was a refugee myself back in 1986 when I *'defected'* from Romania. I spent almost one year in a refugee camp in Traiskirchen, Austria. I know first hand what being a refugee is all about. Me and tens or perhaps hundreds of thousands of other Romanians and Eastern Europeans were fleeing toward West not because we didn't love our countries. Not because we wanted to leave behind parents, relatives, friends, our loved ones' graves, our childhood places. It was because we realized that our children had no future under the oppressive communist regimes. We had no hope - back in 1986- to ever be able see them again. That was a drama for me and my family, not a joy. I have to say -with deep disappointment- that what caused the current humanitarian crisis in the Middle East is the irresponsible policy of the American presidents and Governments. Sadam Hussein was a dictator indeed (I worked for 3 months in Irak in 1986) but the Iraqies had a much better life in their country at that time than we had under Ceausescu. Saddam was not involved in the events of 9/11 2001 and did not have weapons of mass destruction. The war started by the Bush administration in 2003 was a war based on lies, not facts. It was a war for oil. The war destabilized the entire region. The new puppet regime installed by USA in Bagdad started oppressing the sunni minority. This lead to the creation of ISIS. The Irak war and later the disastrous Libya war have created much more terrorists and terrorism than they eradicated. Look at the TV. Irak, Syria, Libya,

Afghanistan all are in ruins. Lots of people die every day in fightings, bombings etc. The poor inhabitants of these countries did not choose freely to leave their land. How can they find food and water, how can they go to work or school, how can they raise children when all day long and all night long they have to hide in order to survive? So let's stop blaming those poor and unfortunate people for which I feel tremendous compassion. The current crisis was not created by them. Europe is paying the price for the USA's mistakes and misjudgments. In Europe, the refugees' cultural and social assimilation is very hard, if not impossible. Nations need to ask USA first, but also other major countries, to spare no effort in order to stop infighting in those counties then stabilize the entire Middle East region so the flux of refugees would eventually stop and hopefully even reverse. Until then this tragedy of huge proportions will continue, with no end in sight, and Europe will primarily pay the price, by having to cope with more millions of hopeless refugees. "

What Mr. Corneliu Lahovari said, with all the vehemence, made us all to forget about the goodies on the table. The deep silence that has been set, including at those connected remotely via Skype, was interrupted by Emy Flora.

-"A few days ago, on the Internet, I read an interview given by a famous American professor. He said in it that the situations created in Iraq, Syria and Libya are actually black holes. The definition given by him is plastic and realistic, I think."

After a new silence, Professor Marius Badescu resumed the talks.

- "I have to appreciate the way the matter is addressed by Mr. Corneliu Lahovari. In particular, because of the fact that he also presents the causes of this tragic phenomenon of vast proportions, as well as the conditions under which he could be resolved."

When I was just wondering why our friendly host (who was usually talkative, to say the least) didn't say anything yet on the subjects in discussion, we heard him taking the floor.

- "Some time ago, I read on the net that Alexis Tsipras, the Prime Minister of Greece, accused western countries of bearing responsibility for the situation in the Middle East that has triggered the migration crisis. He said that the aim was not to introduce democracy, but to serve the financial interests of several rich countries. And now, those who sowed winds are reaping whirlwinds, but these mainly afflict reception countries. He meant first and first Greece."

-. "Sorry to interrupt," said Emy Flora, "but I can not help but show my sincere appreciation for Alexis Tsipras's courage. The whole Greek people acts with courage, in fact. The Greeks were not kneeled by Hitler's German army. They will not surrender to the interests of the wealthy Western countries either. Greece is not Romania! The Greeks will not let the foreigners take under their absolute control all Greece economy. The Greek prime minister is right, saying that we deal with a war of financial interests. And capturing natural resources, I would add. Tsipras asserts that really it is not a matter of exporting democracy, but ultimately some rich and powerful countries try to dominate all the peoples of the world."

It seems that these statements did not please my colleague and friend Adrian Portzan.

- "I don't think the words of Alexis Tsipras and of Emy Flora's are completely politically correct! The Greek Prime Minister has the latitude to say what he wants. I dn't know if this is valid for us who are participating in these discussions."

This time, my friend the Ambassador got angry.

-"If we do not expose our opinions openly, the discourses on such topics of importance will be of no use. I agree with everything that Mr. Emy Flora said. In general terms, also with what Mr.

Corneliu Lahovari said earlier. But after his exposure, I was left with the impression that the former Western colonial powers - Britain, France, Germany, Italy etc. - got less reproaches than they deserve. Really, how could be appreciated, including from a moral point of view, Italy's behavior towards Libya, its former colony during 1911-1943?! On March 27, 2010, at the Arab League summit held in the Libyan city of Sirte, Italian Prime Minister Silvio Berlusconi kissed Muammar Gaddafi's hand. Then, starting on March 11, 2011, Italy participated in the coalition that intervened in Libya; including by allowing planes taking off from the Italian aerodromes to bomb Libya. On October 20, 2011, Libyan leader Muammar Gaddafi was shot."

-"I remember that someone with a developed sense of humor, a black humor of course," interfered Emy Flora, "used for the events in Libya, Tunisia and Egypt the *'North African Spring'* term. Terrible spring, indeed! It will take many years for the three countries to recover completely from the chaos they are currently experiencing."

What he said about Libya, made me take the word too;

-"I think highly of the fact that the Declaration of American Independence *says that* "*all Men are created equal, that they are endowed by their Creator with certain unalienable Rights, that among these are Life, Liberty, and the Pursuit of Happiness...*" I appreciate also very much the fact that the Constitution of the United States starts with the words: "*We the People...*". That's great! But what happened in Libya?! The Libyans got much more *Liberty* than they had during Gaddafi's regime. But there is less *Life* in Libya nowadays, because they were bombed and now they shoot each other. As for the *Pursuit of Happiness*, some of them try to reach the rich countries of Europe; even by rubber boats. Other poor nations are trying to be happy the same way. All those nations are more prolific than the west Europeans... So what will happen in the long run?! Probably my thinking is not politically correct. Shakespeare and Erasmus, and many others, were not politically correct neither. Nevertheless they dared to address those kind of important matters about humane life. But, when Shakespeare wrote: '*To be, or not to be, that is the question...*', there were no atomic or hydrogen bombs, no guided missiles, no Internet... So the same question would be more actual today! World is changing fast (too fast, I guess). Over 45 years ago, when I worked in US, at Valley Forge Industrial Park, I heard American youngsters shouting '*Make love, not war!* '. Today, in the movies

I see on the TV, they don't make love anymore; they make sex. The slogan *'Make sex, not war'*, would be indecent indeed. In 1509 A. D., Erasmus wrote: *'Mars often favors neither side!'* This means that in our supersaturated world with nuclear bombs, the Mars War god could decide that a war between the main countries possessing such weapons would lead to the end of life on the Planet Earth. As in our world there is an huge amount of nuclear arms, those who carry out confrontational foreign policy should remember that."

-"Since we have the pleasure of having a long-standing reputed historian among us -he was a member of the famous Romanian-Hungarian history committee- I would be delighted if he would present his point of view on what I, Mr. Flora and Dan have said" Spoke my friend the Ambassador "I would be glad if you would give your opinion, as well, regarding what happened in Romania in December 89 and after."

-"Being a professional historian, I do know that many years have to pass so that you can really appreciate certain events. These events in Libya, Iraq, Syria and those that have taken place in our country since December 1989 are historically too recent to be able to evaluate them objectively. So I abstain."

-"I am deeply disappointed to hear this. As a host, I would not want to offend Mr. Adrian Portzan, but I think his attitude is related to the lack of courage of many Romanian intellectuals to speak openly on the controversial topics. Especiall if they are related to our situation. Our old Romanian proverb 'the submissed head is not cut by the scimitar' shows its consequences. Perhaps for that reasons too, we Romanians have come to the present situation! Although I am not a historian and I do not have Mr Portzan's professional authority in the matter, I can not help but make a comparison between the events in Libya and those that took place in our country. I believe that if you are really realistic, you can not help but see that they have followed the same scenario. Popular revolt, violence with many dead and injured persons, chaos, the shooting of the dictators... In Romania, the dictator's wife was shot, as well. And in the end, everything that had high value in Libya and in Romania too, came into the possession of several rich and powerful countries. In Libya, the oil and whatever else they have there. In Romania, of course, the oil was also the first to be grabbed. Plus, the natural monopolies of gas, electricity and water distribution, banks and insurance, hypermarkets... Most of the industry - created by sacrificing the living standard of the Romanians-has been really liquidated. Almost all the most really profitable companies, that had not been demolished, came under the possession of the same rich countries. These wealthy countries - in fact, super-rich - with excessively developed industrial capacities, were primarily interested to get the Romanian market. The share of Romanian private companies in the total turnover of all companies active on the local market was 47% in 2015 compared to 49% in foreign companies. The remaining 4% are state-owned companies. Already, 40% of the agricultural land in Romania belongs to foreigners. The Romanian peasants are very poor, so they sell their land at prices ten times lower than in Western countries. You can figure out who the new owners will be. I read in a tourist leaflet that no tree is cut in the Austrian forests. Instead, the Romanian forests are cut wildly till the bare ground by an Austrian company; especially those in Transylvania. They don't give a damn that floods and landslides will follow. Nor to the fact that if deforestation continues at the same pace, Austria being close enough to the places where this robbery takes place, all these consequences will ultimately end up in that country, too."

-"I have to admit that I can't contradict Mr Ionescu's reasoning." Professor Badescu said. "In 1989, the industrial infrastructure available to

Romania has ranked her in the top 10 countries in Europe. This was largely based on technologies, know-how and manufacturing licenses imported from world-renowned companies, in US, Germany, France, England, Canada, Sweden, Japan, and so on. The greatest part of the above mentioned industrial infrastructure was built, during a short historical period, i.e. in 45 years of communist dictatorship. That was done through harsh sacrifice of the Romanians standard of living. It was not done during centuries as happened in various former European colonial powers, where the industrialization process was largely based on the fact that they *'explored, conquered, settled, and exploited large areas of the world'* (the definition of the colonialism, according Encyclopædia Britannica. Those countries got also the needed financial resources by slave trade and using slaves in mines and on the plantations. The Romanians did not have colonies. Actually, they had been the subjects of the wild Ottoman Turks, during several centuries. And that was hundred times worse than living in the colonies of the former European colonial powers. Very little (less than 25%) of the infrastructure existing in Romania in 1989 still has reality today; most of it was *'liquidated'*. The consequence of this fact, was the hardest catastrophe for the Romanians, during all their bimillennial existence. One hundred thirty three years ago, Ion Luca Caragiale -the greatest Romanian playwright- wrote: *'The Romanian industry is admirable, is sublime we may say, but it is completely non-existent.'* To the same reality we are back today! There was a extended deindustrialisation. In the following fields, the manufacturing have disappeared or have been reduced to minimum: electrotechnical, electronics, automation, fine mechanics, bearings, optics, tractors, locomotives, wagons, ships, oil and mining equipment, furniture, cement, paints and varnishes, textiles (spinning, weaving, knitting, garments), glassware, shoes, sugar, oil, meat and milk products, medicines etc. For example, in the year of 1980, in Romania were produced 70,873 tractors, 481 thousands tons dead weight marine vessels, 601 passenger railway cars, 276 diesel and electric locomotives; today their production is zero. Though this country has the second most fertile agricultural land in Europe (after France), it gave up completely tractors manufacturing! No computers and peripheral equipments are manufactured in Romania today, neither. The vast majority of research and development institutes and agricultural research stations have been abolished. State agricultural and agricultural mechanization enterprises have been dismantled.

The irrigation system, built with money borrowed from the World Bank, has been destroyed almost entirely; for the reimbursement of the borrowed money the Romanians have sacrificed their standard of living during decades. Have been abandoned the programs to combat soil erosion and desertification, as well as the continuation of work on the Siret-Danube or Bucharest-Danube canals."

-"I agree hundred percent with all your remarks Professor Badescu; and with those of Mr Ionescu also." My friend Emy Flora said. "I just read the book published by you and Mr. Dragos entitled *The End of History as Such and Neoliberalism Forever?! And Case Study: Romania After 22 Years of Neoliberalism*. I have it with me and I would like to cite from it the following passage: 'A synthetic definition, including the causes that brought this country in its present situation is given by one of the greatest contemporary Romanian historians who stated that: '*The post-December political class is the most incompetent, the most greedy and arrogant in Romanian history. Lacking expertise, hungry for money-making and secure of impunity, this political class fell on Romania with only one thought: to get rich. They have robbed (the country); even more than the much blamed phanariots did. Today, we see that the industry is liquidated, the agriculture is crashed to the ground, the health system is in collapse, the education is in crisis, Romania' international individuality has disappeared.'* In your book you say that 'The comparison with the *much blamed phanariots*, i.e. with those sent in the old times by the Turkish Sultans to administer the Romanian Principalities, is entirely realistic.' I believe that the respective historian correctly synthesizes the situation in which Romania is today. As Mr Adrian Portzan said that we can refer to anything we choose, I would like to read some additional quotes -that I highly appreciate- from the same book. Here it is! 'The fact that mankind has reached a critical moment, results also from the following quotes from some of the great thinkers. Thus, Albert Einstein said: *We shall require a substantially new manner of thinking if mankind is to survive.* At the end of last century, Loren C. Eiseley said: *If the human race is to survive into the next century, scientific technology will have to learn how to control the devastating forces it has unwittingly turned loose on the planet - the world's exploding population, the reckless pollution of the environment, the spiraling arms race and the expenditure of irreplaceable energy.* Noam Chomsky said: *If we continue to produce energy by combustion, the human race isn't going to survive much.'* Any rational men would agree hundred percent with those quotes."

-"We published the book -in English and Romanian- at the request of Professor Anghel Rugina. In it we have presented also, directly and openly (not only implicitly), what are the absolutely necessary solutions, without which the situation of Romania can not be remedied. On the contrary, for ordinary Romanians it will be more and more difficult to survive. In case the status quo is maintained in this country, I think that the most competitive and capable Romanians will emigrate; which in fact means the gradual dissolution of Romania as a country. The *optimistic and politically correct* views that the Romanians have always managed to survive the difficulties of the past and will do it in the future too etc, is wishful thinking. This kind of thinking is like the following funny saying of George Bernard Shaw: *'There are two tragedies in life. One is to lose your heart desire. The other is to gain it'*. Unfortunately the decision makers don't believe that the actual situation of this country is grave; in fact they don't care, because all of them became overnight rotten rich."

-"I present my apologies, again!" Emy Flora said. "I feel obliged to make a comparison; I do that because I am the oldest of the participants in these discussions, and I was one of the direct witnesses of Romania's entire industrialization process. This industrialization began shortly after the Second

World War, by the Romanian-Soviet joint ventures called *Sovroms*."

- "That is a crazy statement." Exclaimed Adrian Portzan. "We will start now to glorify the *Sovroms* joint ventures; of which even the communist rulers of Romania tried very hard to get rid off. Do you want re-affirm the liar slogan of that time that *Sovroms* represented brotherly help from the Soviet Union?!"

"To say such a thing would be stupid. A big untruth! The reality is that, in the first years after the Second World War, the Soviet Union was deeply interested in the industrial development of the satellite countries -or the popular democracies as they called themselves at the time. That was due to the fact that the war had destroyed the infrastructure and industrial capabilities of the most developed part of USSR. In addition, 27 million soviet people died in the war. Most of them were former workers and all kind of industry technicians and experts. As our friendly host said, 25-26 years ago it was the other way around! The Western world victorious in the Cold War -had overdeveloped industrial capabilities, some of which were partially used. The truth is that, in the period in which Romania was a satellite country of USSR, Romanian industry and economy evolved quite fast; with great sacrifices for most of the

Romanians, certainly. After 1989, Romania came under the protection of the Western Democracies, and you saw what followed. Ilie Serbanescu - a well-known economist - even published a book titled *'Romania a Colony on the Outskirts of Europe'* What can you say about all that happened?!"

Adrian Portzan protested again.

-"That's amazing! In 21st century, you are praising the Soviet Union and the Stalinist industrialization. Even the Russians, years ago, have revealed Stalin's crimes and his so called 'personality cult'. It seems that you forgot all that happened. The Russians themselves know better than you do!"

-"You are right; the Russians themselves know better. I just read on the Internet that *Levada Center* conducted a poll between April 7 and 10, 2017, on a sample of 1,600 people, in which the respondents could choose multiple variants at the same time. According to the survey, 38% of Russians believe that Stalin is the most important personality of all time. Stalin is followed shortly by Vladimir Putin (34%), who is on the same footing as the poet Pushkin, The first leader of the Soviet Union, Vladimir Lenin, was ranked fourth in the preferences of the Russians, with 32%, and Peter I ranked fifth with 29%. The first foreigner in the top is Napoleon I, on the 14th place, with 9%. Five years ago, the survey was showing the following ranking: Stalin, Peter I, Lenin, Pushkin and Putin."

-"That's crazy! Stalin ranked first, after he harmed and caused pain to so many Russians?!"

-"Yes… But, many Russians believe that Stalin did not hurt Russia. On the contrary, they believe that the rapid Stalinist industrialisation saved *Россия Мать*. Otherwise, Hitler would have defeated Russia and would have liquidated Russia and so many, many Russians."

-"I can see that you are a Russophile."

-"I am neither a Russophile nor a Russophobe. Maybe, I appreciate all nations according to the cultural benefits I got from each of them. I enjoyed American movies -Casablanca and many others-, Hair and Jesus Christ Superstar Musicals, Metropolitan Opera Performances, Mark Twain and other great writers… So, you could say that I am an Americanophile. I love Dostoyevsky, Tolstoy, Pasternak, Tchaikovsky etc. The same way I love the French, English cultures -first and first the unique Shakespeare…I am a Hungarian, but I love Eminescu, Caragiale and many others… But, enough with my digressions! They were caused by the fact that quite a few of the intellectuals in our country became Russophobe overnight. This way, they believe that can prove that are truly anticommunists"

My friend the Ambassador took the floor.

-"I would like to refer again to the problems of our country. Amazingly, Romania is the only country in the world that has destroyed its own economy to such an extent. The Romanian commercial fleet (one of the largest in the world) and ocean fishing fleet (the second one in the Atlantic Ocean after the Soviet fleet) were volatilized. Also, there were sold to foreigners all the natural resources, namely oil, gold, rare metals, shale gas etc. Slowly, land is bought by foreigners. Forests are grazed to the ground and exported in the form of logs and timber."

A new silence followed, which was interrupted eventually by Professor Badescu.

-"Mr Lahovari also addressed the issue of the causes that determined the scale of the refugee phenomenon. He rightly defined it as a 'tragedy of huge proportions'. Ms. Kate Shagall also referred to the causes. I say we should deepen this matter."

-"But the whole problem has not yet been exposed." I said. "Nothing was said about the exodus of millions of inhabitants of the Eastern European countries, including Romania. In the email I sent to my friend Herman, I added a supplementary viewpoint. I have here a hard copy of that email. That addition is the following: 'In your recent email, you wrote that your children will probably stay in the USA for the rest of their lives. My only son intends to remain in the USA also. He knows that wages in Romania are 7 or 8 times lower than wages in USA or in Austria. I remember that in the seventies, when both of us were employed in Vienna by the same American multinational corporation, you preferred to work in Austria. As you were the best salesman in Vienna subsidiary, you had the possibility to work in Minneapolis. And during that time the wages in USA were much higher than in Austria. Today the wages in USA and in Austria are quite close. At that time, I believed in the following old Romanian saying: *Although the bread is bad, it is better to get it in your own country.* I don't know if that saying makes sense in English. In Romanian language, this saying, makes sense. Today, the youngsters of this country believe in the ancient Latin expression, *ubi bene ibi patria,* meaning that the fatherland is in the country where the life is good. Do you think that our children are right, or ourselves?' What do you have to say to all that Herman?"

-"OK, I am ready to give the answer now." Herman Prashunder said. "Basically the situation of our children has not changed much. Our son is still in Florida and is now teaching Mathematics as Professor at the private Kaiser University in Tampa. Our daughter is at university in New York for another year on a stipendium. I see it pragmatic. It is their life and I don't think I should persuade them to change their decision. We will only live a few more years, but they have to live with their decision several decades. It is true, I never wanted to move to the USA in my younger years although I admired that country very much; at this time I would not see any reason to move to USA neither."

-"Mr. Herman Prashunder's approaches are particularly interesting," said Professor Badescu. "I think that his pragmatic view is logical; it is normal for the young people themselves to decide what they will do, since they are the ones who will endure for many years the consequences of those decisions. It is also important that he is finding out that the proportions of different ethnicities in the Western European countries are changing too, not only by massive arrivals of more prolific populations from outside of the continent, but also by the fact that some of their own citizens - especially young people- emigrate; especially to America."

-"The proportions of different ethnicities change in our country, too." My friend the Ambassador exclaimed. "The percentage of the Romanians declines. The Roma people -others call them Romani people- are growing steadily; they are much more prolific. In 40-50 years from now, their ethnic group will be a majority in Romania."

-"This is a stupid projection! I am sorry to say that. As, a historian I can't see what are your arguments, or which are the statistical data you base your assumption."

-"I have no statistical data. But, I will give you a concrete argument. A few days ago, I was traveling with a public bus in Bucharest. With the same bus was traveling a family of Roma people with their six children; one was still a baby, the oldest looked to be 10-12 old. The husband, his wife and their children were not wearing those specific colorful clothes, but luxury western style garments."

-"That is a shallow argument."

-"OK! I will give you other argument too. In the period since December 1989, millions of the most competitive Romanian citizens (between 4 or 5 millions; nobody knows their exact number) have gone to gain their living in the wider world. They have even reached Latin America, Japan and Australia. The rate of economic migration in Romania is the highest in the world. Between 2000 and 2015 it was 7.3% per year (according to the United Nations estimate). This rhythm is overtaken only by migration from Syria, whose **Diaspora** grew by 13% per year due to the civil war. Even now, when we are talking and having this excellent dinner, between 9 and 12 Romanian citizens are leaving this country every hour for good. In 2007 - the year in which our country joined European Union- 544,074 Romanian citizens emigrated. That is, 62 Romanians per hour! Today, the Romanians in Spain form the largest group of foreigners in that country, having surpassed Moroccans in 2007."

-"Among the Romanian citizens who left our country, there were Roma people too."

-"That's right! But years ago, from France and Germany, the Roma people used to be sent back to Romania. The issue of the Romanians emigration is complex, so I hope that we will refer to it later on. In addition to what I said about the fact that the percentage of the Romanians declines, we have to keep in mind that nowadays some of the companies in this country intend to employ employees from Vietnam, Pakistan, Philippine etc. For example, they mean to bring welders from those countries, because they accept even lower salaries than in Romania. Also, we see that a lot of Muslims settle in our country for economic reasons. In addition, the refugee quota that has been allocated to our country by the European Union will also come. It is said that Turkey had obtained the agreement of the Romanian government to build a mosque in Bucharest that will be the largest in the entire European Union. It was been told that it would also have facilities for studying Islam by thousands of students. The entire activity of the respective mosque is to be done in a language and a writing known by very few Romanians. What is the real purpose of Turkey in building this gigantic mosque?! It seems that Turkey will never forget that the old Romanian countries have been under Turkish yoke for hundreds of years! It is obvious that in the last period, profiting of its strong industrialization and the vertiginous growth of its population, Turkey is trying to become again a hegemonic power in this geographical area! I read in some old statistics, that before World War 2, Turkey had 14 million inhabitants (compared to 19 million in existence that time in Romania), reaching today to nearly 80 million. It is estimated that over 50-70 years, there will be more Turks in the world than Russians. Turkish President Recep Tayyip Erdogan has called on Turks living in Europe: *'Go live in better neighborhoods. Drive the best cars. Live in the best houses. Make not three, but five children. Because you are the future of Europe.'* That means that nowadays the demographic weapon is used, as well; not just the scimitar as they did centuries ago. In case Turkey will manage to enter in the European

Union, Europe will become more *'Turkish'* and it will adept to Islam fast. In such a case, our European ladies will no longer be able to expose their legs and navel on the street; their face will be covered, so that only their eyes could be seen. According to *sharia* law, for concubinage, they will be stoned until they are dead. The gays will no longer be able to take advantage of the current democratic laws to marry each other. Nor will they be able to adopt the children of non-homosexuals."

-"Nowadays, the Caucasians or Caucasoids of Europe are interested just to have fun. They don't think about the future." Emy Flora said. "The white rase forgot that in the Bible (Genesis 1:28), is written: 'God blessed them; and God said to them, 'Be fruitful and multiply, and fill the earth, and subdue it; and rule over the fish of the sea and over the birds of the sky and over every living thing that moves on the earth.' God desired for Adam and Eve to have many children. As far as I know, the gays can not produse no children; not even with the help of the up to day modern technology."

After awhile the Ambassador Ionescu continued with his speech.

-"Unlike the extraordinary economic results, achieved by Turkey over the past 25 years, our country has suffered a brutal deindustrialisation and the population has declined steadily. We have come to have the population of the year of 1960. Birth rate has fallen enormously. As I said, millions of Romanians left their homeland; most of them work in the rich EU countries. It was and it is a real exodus. In case that this exodus will continue (and most probably it will), soon enough, more Romanians will make their living abroad than in Romania. In that case, in the long run, eventually all Romanians will work abroad; in this country will remain only controversial people like Gigi Becali, Hrebenciuc, Miky the Bribe, Vanghelie, Vântu and others like them, whose names I don't dare to pronounce."

-"You forgot a certain lady friend of a former President of our Republic, that used to be the most important minister in the Romanian Government; actually, she was the *de facto* Prime Minister. As she became divorcée from a rich old man, she got a new boyfriend and then a husband - a real strong and young fisherman from the Danube Delta- so, she will not abandon this country neither."

-"You interrupted me again Mr. Flora. But that's OK, as you are always right… In the rich EU countries, most of the Romanians work in menial jobs in constructions and agriculture. I do not blame them; wages are many times higher there. For example, in Bucharest, monthly wages of the employees of hypermarkets are around 300 euros. In Hamburg and Paris, wages are 7 or 8 times higher. Though the productivity of all those employees in Romania and in the Western countries is quite the same, and the hypermarkets are owned by the same German and French companies."

At this point, Mrs. Kate Shagall intervened.

-"The topic just talked about is exciting. I mean, what happened with the Romanian industry... There were a lot of uneconomic factories in Romania because of the communist system, but there were some good things as well and as far as I can see, they've been sold or scrapped and Romania is now an economic colony. This was with the assent of your politicians though I'm not quite sure they saw exactly what was happening. Now, I have a question for you gentlemen. I am curious as to why Romanians might want to travel to the US on a visitor visa then remain illegally and work when they can go work legally in the EU. Do you have any idea?"

Ambassador Ionescu offered to give the answer again..

-"There are several reasons... I assume that you know that the Romanians are the most *Americanophile* nation of the world. To prove that it is enough to quote what *President Nixon* said, on his departure from Romania, in August 3, 1969: '*It has been my privilege to visit over 60 countries in the world, and of all the countries I have visited, there has been none that has been more memorable than the visit to Romania. This is… true also because of the wonderfully heartwarming welcome we have received from the people of Romania every place we have gone.*' He was most warmly greeted, because he was the President of United States!"

-"It is very true that Romanians regard America as a kind of Promised Land." I said. "I will tell you a little story. After five years and two months I worked abroad for an American Corporation, I returned to the Institute of Computer Engineering (ITC) in Bucharest. One of my old colleagues set up a club called "*Club Felix*", after the name of the Romanian computers produced under French license. Every Saturday, various writers and well-known people were invited to present exposures to the club. I remember that at the beginning of 1976, a few months after my return to the country, I participated in a meeting in which an interesting exposure was presented by Marin Sorescu at Felix Club. He was already appreciated as one of the greatest Romanian poets. For the next Saturday, my old friend, who was also head of the 'Felix Club,' proposed me to present an exposure titled

'America Saw by a Romanian.' Of course I have accepted, preparing the most interesting Kodak slides that I have shot throughout all United States. To my surprise, when I arrived at the Felix Club, the big hall in which the exposure was about to take place was full. There were at least three times more people than at Marin Sorescu's exposure. Obviously, it was not because of me, an nobody, but due to the subject regarding America. The discussions were heated. One wondered if I thought he could face the competition in America. I replied, 'I have graduated the University many years before you; at that time we did not know much about computers. So, if I was able to face the competition, you would not have any problem with the adaptation.' A few months later, that guy who was Jewish, left this country for Germany; some of his relatives had paid for the approval to the Romanian state 8,000 West Germans marks (that is $3.050). Later on he went to US. In the following days, one of the best-qualified lady expert in the institute told me in great secrets: 'You had a job in Philadelphia and you came back to the ITC in Bucharest! That was quite stupid my friend!' She pronounced the Philadelphia as if she was talking about the heavenly paradise. The same reproach was addressed to me by some other lady colleague from ITC. It turned out that women were more fearless than the men; the men colleagues considered that, at the time, such a discussion was too risky."

-"I think we have to go back to deepening the causes," Professor Badescu said. "Perhaps we should also take into account the fact that millions of millions of immigrants arrived in Europe from outside the continent, long before the military campaigns in Iraq, Afghanistan, Libya and Syria. Who wants to present his opinion?"

Emy Flora seemed willing to intervene.

-"The wave of immigrants began with the decolonization of Asia and Africa. In my opinion, the first Asians and Africans established in Great Britain, France, Belgium etc., were those who worked closely with the colonial authorities. After the liberation from colonialism, in order to escape the possible retaliation from their fellow countrymen, they opted for the way of emigration to the former metropolis. Another cause is related to the dramatic decrease in the birth rate of the white race (the race of those called caucasians by the Americans), simultaneously with the excessive development of the economy in the rich western countries. The growing demand for labor could no longer be met by the local people, so the import of non-European employees was used."

-"Emy is perfectly right!" I said. "At the beginning of the 1980's, I negotiated a contract for the creation of a Romanian-West German joint venture for the manufacture of mechanized mining equipment. In the end, the joint venture was not approved because Ceausescu appreciated that the existing one at Resita - with a German company - was sufficient. When the German company owner took me through several of his factories, I found that almost all of the workers I tried to exchange a few words with knew neither German nor English. Asking for clarification, I was told that most of the workers of that factory were Turks, brought from Turkey. So, the Western countries have resorted to this solution, simply because it was in their interest to do so."

-"Yes, that it is so!" Emy said. "It should be added that at that time the existence of the *'iron curtain'* made it impossible to import labor from the so-called *'socialist camp'*. The current migration of the most competitive part of the East European labor force to West Europe is particularly advantageous for rich Western countries. For the former so called 'socialist countries', the consequences are catastrophic. After spending their tiny financial funds for schooling, the best-prepared East Europeans go to the rich countries to enrich the rich."

-"I can not contradict my friend Emy." I said. "In connection with what he said, I have in mind a particularly significant and serious case of brain drain. Some time ago, a minister in our government declared on TV that only 1% of Romanian high school students who were awarded International Olympiad medals (in math, ICT, physics, chemistry, etc.) are returning to work in this country. But let the orator continue his exposure."

-"Speaking of Romania, I gather that just now there is an uproar over the revelations of Sebastian Ghita. Have you gentlemen heard anything?" Mrs Shagall asked.

-"To this question," said Ambassador Ionescu, "I will answer the same way Zorba replies in the novel of Kazantzakis: *'You think too much and ask such sensible questions.'* Though I think that I just waste my time, I think too much on those kind of matters too. All I know about Sebastian Ghita, is what was said on the Internet and on the TV. In short, he used to be a basketball player. Years ago, he was elected a member of the Romanian Parliament. Following public ICT contracts worth hundreds of millions of euros, his fortune vas estimated by Forbes at around €100 million. Some of the millions payrd to Ghita were through fake IT acquisitions services contracts. It is obvious that you know quite well what is said, on the TV and the Internet, about the corruption in this country in general. If only half of those are true, that means that the number of crooks per capita here is higher than in any other country member of European Union. The stupid crooks are less dangerous than the clever crooks. In case all those are just common crooks, they are almost harmless compared to politician-crooks or to those occupying high decision-making positions. Here, these kind of crooks became very very rich. For example, a well known polititician, before being put in jail, said that he was *'the poorest politician in Romania'* (on the Internet was shown that he has only a bit over one million euros in his bank accounts). He declared also that he was innocent. In this country, absolutely all high ranking crooks that were put in jail, are innocent like newborn babies. They keep most of their fortune too. Though some of them can't write, they publish books and so they get out sooner from the jail. On the TV was said that, one certain crook (he was in UE parlament and a candidate in the election for the Romanian President) built churches and a book was published! On the Internet you can find the businesses by which politicians became rich and how they try very hard to 'improve' the laws, in order to be more lenient. And they may succed!

Most of them have colorfull life: one had 5 wifes; one after the other, he does not have a harem yet. Regarding Sebastian Ghita there were a lot of stories on the TV and Internet. About two years ago, the existing Prime Minister that time and his friend Sebastian Ghita took a trip together to Dubai. In just one evening they spent, in Cavalli Club, *"2,700 Euros (six months working for a medical doctor in Romania) for some mineral water, a 21-year Chivas and champagne"*. Like all the other very rich politicians, Mr Sebastian Ghita says that he is innocent like newborn babies. Maybe! But, why the bloody hell did he travel with the Prime Minister to Dubai?! Why not let him home, to work for the Romanian people who made him Prime Minister? Maybe, they knew that not the Romanian people made him Prime Minister, but his political friends, including guys like Mr Ghita."

At this point Daniel Dragoş Jr intervened in the discussions; he had not yet spoken.

-"Being the youngest of the participants in these discussions, I have a lot to learn and little to say. I came to America for a better life. The Declaration of Independence annexed to the Constitution of the United States speaks of 'the Pursuit of Happiness' and 'Liberty.' One of my American friends, who managed to get a good financial situation, told me that in the world of today, man is free only and only if he has money. So I'm working hard to make money. But, that friend of mine told me that if you are not an Einstein in your field of activity, you can earn much money only from the work of others. That means you need to have as many employees as possible to work for you. Unfortunately, I'm not an Einstein, nor have I ever managed to have a company in which others work for me. Just the same, I try my best to be happy."

-"Gentlemen, most you said is exciting." Mrs Shagall said. "As for happiness... it is much overblown these days. Happiness is great but perhaps quiet satisfaction in life is better."

-"I think, "Emy said," that there is no truth in the well-known and wonderful slogan of the French Revolution *Liberté, égalité, fraternité*. This was demonstrated by what has been said here. Nowadays, the inequality between nations and people has reached inhuman proportions. In the face of interest, even brothers' fraternity fades."

The face of my friend the Ambassador was a big smile, which meant that he was 100% in agreement with what was said.

-"Quite often, I keep asking myself if the humanity actually evolved from this point of view. One of the earliest Latin playwright Maccius Plautus (254 – 184 BC) said in one of his plays: *'A person is a wolf toward other person, no man knows when he is not.'* The original abridged form   is:

'Homo homini lupus est'. Later on, Jesus said: 'Love your neighbor as yourself.' The Declaration of Independence (July 4, 1778) says: We hold these truths to be self-evident, that all men are created equal, that they are endowed by their Creator with certain unalienable Rights, that among these are Life, Liberty and the pursuit of Happiness.' La devise de la Révolution française (July 14, 1789): 'Liberté, Égalité, Fraternité!' 'The Communist Manifesto' (1848) of Marx and Engels, summarises the theories about the nature of society and politics, that in their own words is: 'The history of all hitherto existing society is the history of class struggles'. Samuel P. Huntington's theory (1993) is: 'The clash of civilizations will dominate global politics.' President Trump's Poland Speech (July 2917): West's fight against 'radical Islamic terrorism' was necessary to protect 'our civilization and our way of life.' 'The fundamental question of our time is whether the west has the will to survive… I could give other quotes, too."

-"I can't follow you." Adrian Portzan said. "What is the meaning of all those quotes picked up from I don't know which books?"

-"That's a good question! I will answer that. First, I have to tell you that I picked up most of those quotes from the *net;* namely, from Wikipedia. The question is whether the human nature has changed or not after two thousand and two hundred years; that is, from the time of Plautus until today. I tend to believe that the answer is negative! Let's consider the illustration in Huntington's book, regarding the -*'more conflictual or less conflictual'*- contradictions between West, Islam, Sinic, Ortodox (Russia), Japan, Hindu (India), Latin America and Africa. Actually, from that illustration we can see that by clashes of civilizations, Huntington means clashes between nations or countries. So, if Plautus would live today, he could say: *'A country is behaving like a wolf toward other country, no man knows when a certain country will not behave in that way.'* Nowadays, not just a *'person is a wolf toward other person'*, but nations behave the same way. Marx and Engels theory 'of class struggles' between the rich and the poor, became obsolete. Everybody admires the rich and tries to become rich themselves too, by all means. We believe in Jesus, but few of us follow his teachings."

-"Would you," Adrian Portzan asked "go and *'sell all your possessions and give the money to the poor, and you will have treasure in heaven. Then come, follow me.'* That's what Jesus said."

-"Frankly, the answer is no. I became rich just recently, so I prefer to enjoy being rich for a while."

-"Do you see, it's easy to give away the possessions of others. That is what the rich countries believe too... C'est la vie!"

-"Then what is the solution?!" Professor Badescu exclaimed. "Some people do live like in a real paradise. At the same time, the great majority of them do live like in a real hell. Where are the ethics and the morality?!..."

-"The situation is not that tragic." Emy Flora said, with ironic smile on his face. "Quite a lot of people do live somehow better than in inferno, namely they live like in the purgatory. In addition to that, those who take it hard in this world will go to paradise in the other world. They look forward to die and to be happy in heavens."

-"Due especially to the evolution in the rich countries," I said, "the existing consumer society can not be sustained for long in the years to come, because of the real material possibilities of the planet and of the accelerated environmental pollution as well. Recently, I attended an academic seminar, in which it was said that the current American consumer society would be possible only if our planet had at most one billion inhabitants. The West European consumer society would be possible for up to 3 billion inhabitants. But, now more than 7 billion people live on earth; compared to 1.6 billion at the beginning of the last century!"

At this point of time, my friend the Ambassador took the floor.

-"I want to return to what is said in Dan's email. I do know that those who came from the former colonies, and their descendants as well, who live in Western countries will not love the native white people. Actually, once they settle in the Western countries, they will be *de facto* a kind of *fifth-column*. That is so, because the new arrivals will be marginalized and, for years, they will be much poorer than the natives. The terrorists -some of them born in the West and being citizens of Western Europe- commit terrible atrocities in the territories occupied by the so-called ISIS state. Terrible terrorist acts took place in France, Great Britain, Germany, Belgium etc. There is a real terrorist war going on. As a result, responsible people in the West declared that, as a counter-measure a ruthless war was started against international terrorism."

"I discussed this matter with an Arab friend of mine." Emy Flora said. "He is businessman married to a Romanian woman. He told me *'just put yourself in their shoes. They do not have aircraft carriers or submarines, no cruise missiles, no drones, no fighter-bombers, no other such civilized means of waging war, so they fight as they can and with the means they have.'* It seams, that the outcome of this war is uncertain. Their number does not diminish in time. Their religion is younger, being at he stage where Christians were singing hymns of glory in the Colosseum, while the packs of lions rushed to devour them. The terrorists with explosive, that blow themselves up in the midst of what they see as their enemies, hope that they will be martyrs in the heavens and that they will be rewarded. That is, if we really would want to see how it really is. Sure, I agree with Mr. Herman Prashunder that *'we old people will not feel the changes in our lifetime so much.'* But the situation could change if the terrorists will be able to get atomic weapons. In that case, the danger would grow enormously, as the terrorists have a total disdain for people's lives, and because they do not lack amateurs to sacrifice their lives in terrorism. What do you think of the reasoning of my Arab friend?! "

-"What do I think?" Adrian Portan said annoyed. "Terrorists are terrorists!"

-"At last you have an opinion. That's great!"

My friend the Ambassador said.

Hearing what my friends said, I thought I should continue in the same way.

-"I do like the sincerity of the speakers. I'll try to do the same. I hope to succeed. I read, on the net, various quotes from Martin Luther King. In one of them, he blames *'the white supremacy'*. He was referring to the United States, indeed.. I want to refer to the *'white supremacy'* that has existed, during centuries, all over the globe. Many positive things can be attributed to that historical period. In ancient Greece the philosophy flourished and the democracy emerged! The civilization of ancient Rome followed. In the Renaissance, art and culture have received fantastic development. Today's civilization is largely created by *'the white supremacy'*. The current civilization related to computers and ICT has emerged and originally developed in the US, and then spreading around the world. But the *"white supremacy"* is also responsible for long and bloody wars. The Hundred Years' War, The Thirty Years' War, the Napoleonic wars... The two world wars were started by white race countries. The *'white supremacy'* is also linked to the colonization of the Americas, Africa, Asia and Australia. Some of the native populations have been practically liquidated. According to the history course mentioned in the email that is the subject of our discussions, the initial accumulations for the industrialization of the West were based on the plunder of natural resources in the Americas, Asia and Africa, on the work of slavery in the colonies and the slave trade. What lessons can you draw from all this?"

Again my friend Adrian Portan was dissatisfied with my words.

- "Being just an engineer by training you are not qualified to address such a historical subject."

-"Although I am neither a historian nor a strategist," my friend the Ambassador said, "I think I have the right to refer to aspects of the evolution of human society. Some developments in the past and nowadays seem to me to support my views. For example, one of the crusades launched by the West-European Catholic world, with the aim to release the Holy Land, passing through Constantinople, has robbed pitilessly the capital of Orthodox Christianity. Napoleon was not entirely satisfied, though he had taken under his control an important part of Europe. So he started his adventure in Russia. The result is known. Hitler did the same; with much bigger losses; and dozens of million deaths. The two sides of the Cold War were largely made up of countries that were also part of the same white race. Apparently, the great winner in the Cold War was United States. Do the Americans live better than before this victory?! From my discussions with American friends, it turned out that in order for an ordinary family to carry it as well as before, it is necessary for both spouses to have a job. Before, for the same standard of living, it was enough only for the husband to have a job. The percentage of the white people in the world population is in a worrying fall. In spite of all these and of the fact that the European Communist regimes succumbed in East Europe, an economic and propagandistic war is unfolding inside the white race, i.e. between the West and Russia. The spending against each other in this propagandistic war and the military spending of each side are on the rise. After the First World War, *'the sanitary cordon'* against Soviet Russia, namely from the Baltic Sea to the Black Sea, was created. Nowadays, some would like this *'sanitary cordon'* to be moved even closer to Moscow. On February 7, 1945, when any rational man realized that Germany had lost the war, Hitler said emphatically: *'It is eastwards, only and always eastwards, that is the veins of our race must expand, that.is the direction in which the expansion of our German race must take place. It is the direction Nature intended for the expanses of the German people.'* The old *'Drang nach Osten'* of the Germans has again became actual."

At this point, Emy Flora spoke again.

--"I read somewhere that, close to the end of the Second World War, Hitler has come to the conclusion that, as a rule, advanced and civilized nations are being defeated by the more backward nations. Maybe, Hitler came to this view, knowing that the backward nations had conquered the Roman and Byzantine empires."

-"Maybe… But let us go back to the nowadays *'Drang nach Osten'* Russian officials declared that in the event of a direct military attack against Russia, they are determined to retaliate with all their nuclear weapons. Such an eventuality could lead to the end of life on earth. This danger arises from the fact that there are huge nuclear and thermonuclear weapons (almost 16,000) in the world, about 94% of which belong to the United States and to the Russian Federation. In addition, the two countries have huge quantities of plutonium in their deposits, which can be quickly converted into thousands of atomic bombs. Unfortunately, some rulers do play with the fate of all of us. Who will benefit, in the long run, from the confrontation between Russia and the West?! In any case, the countries with Caucasian populations will not benefit! Especially because both sides are in a disastrous demographic decline! In addition, it is not taken into account the fact that, due to the brutal decline of its population, Russia has no real prospects to regain a superpower status."

Corneliu Lahovari said: "As an American citizen I am concerned about what happens in US. In 1971, the proportion between the average income of an employee and of a company CEO with more than 1,000 employees was in the United States of about 1 to 50. Today this ratio has reached 1 to over 500. Also, I read on the net that in 20 oct. 2015, Credit Suisse Bank stated that: with just $10 'you are wealthier than 25% of Americans. The same bank estimated that a large chunk of Americans and Europeans have a negative net worth. This means that they have no money; but actually they have to pay off the credit cards debts and their bank loans. In the capitalist countries, the situation of the middle class began to degrade immediately after the collapse of the Iron Curtain and the dismemberment of the USSR. This was due to the fact that it has disappeared the 'pressure' exerted on capitalism to maintain a high standard of living for the middle class, and thus to avoid the socialism becoming attractive."

- "Yes, you are right; that's how it is." Mrs. Kate Shagall said. "And I think it's not good that wealth is focused on the very few. One of the things that has happened in the U.S. over the past thirty or forty years is the concentration of wealth in the hands of fewer and fewer people at the top while other people are less and less well off. The way this has been done, on the whole, is to give a few managers, along with stockholders, bigger and bigger *compensation packages* (salary plus other benefits, the other benefits to avoid taxes) and to take those benefits, including wage levels, away from the works. For instance, my cousin has worked for a caterer for fifteen years but she doesn't get a salary. She is a *'contractor'* (this is illegal but people still do it) which means that she has to pay both the employee's and the employer's share of Social Security and Medicare taxes. Additionally, she has no regular sick leave, no vacation (though they do *'give'* her some time off) and no security whatsoever. A very large portion of American workers are in this position. Another ploy is that workers are only hired *'when needed'*. Computers forecast needs; the worker has to stay available to work but has no guarantee of work. For all of these people and more, income is not enough to cover expenses in many cases unless a couple is married and both contribute. So more and more goes on the credit card."

- "All you said is very, very interesting." Professor Badescu said. "Most of the Romanians believe that all you Americans are millionaires.

- "Living is often difficult in the U.S. these days, especially about housing and a lot of people live on credit cards which is, to be honest, a bad thing to do because the interest rate is high. Sometimes it's because they just spend too much money; sometimes it's because there is no alternative. If your salary is, say, $4,500 take home pay a month (which is higher than average) and you have bought a house with a mortgage payment of $2,500 a month or more but now can't split that with a wife, then electricity and so forth run as high as $500 a month, put in another $400 a month for a car payment, $300 a month for house taxes and insurance and $200 a month for gas to go to work -this is just off the top of my head but not unreasonable. You are down to $600 a month for food and all your other expenses which isn't enough. And sometimes selling a house isn't the answer because prices go up and down but in many case -especially if the house was purchased before 2008 -the selling price is now less than the original purchase price. Many, many people in the US are in this situation and most don't earn even as much as my theoretical person in this exercise. It's one of the reasons that Trump and Bernie Sanders have been so popular. The rich have rigged the system so that they benefit at the expense of everyone else and people are hurting. It's a little intrusive, after all, how things are. Not only the gap between the rich and the poor is continuously increasing, the few concentrate more and more power. To be elected, you need enormous electoral funds. Those with a lot of money can create hazards for the environment as well. Let me tell you a concrete case related to the place where I live. It's a small California town. People with lots of money put their eyes on a beautiful area in the town. They want to build luxurious homes there."

The comments of Mrs. Kate Shagall made me take the floor. "On November 2, 1970, I started to work in Valley Forge Industrial Park, Pennsylvania. All my friends, working with me in research and development, looked to be quite happy. They were well-to-do, although all their wives were not employed; they were just housewives. I ask myself if those sort of employees are that happy today. One American friend of mine told me that, nowadays in United States, to have the standard of living existing in the seventies, both you and your wife have to work. One single job in a common family is not enough nowadays.

- "You my high school colleague Dan, you are a born pessimist. I am not sure that Mrs. Kate Shagall is hundred percent right, neither. I know that USA is the most powerful country in the world and is the only superpower nowadays." Adrian Portzan said.

Again, what he said irritated me, so I retaliated.

-"To prove that the opinions of Mrs. Kate Shagall are correct I will give the following excerpts from President Trump Inauguration Address: *For too long a small group in our nation's capital has reaped the rewards of government while the people have borne the cost. Washington flourished but the people did not share in its wealth. Politicians prospered but the jobs left and the factories closed. The establishment protected itself but not the citizens of our country. Their victories have not been your victories. Their triumphs have not been your triumphs. While they have celebrated there has been little to celebrate for struggling families all across our land.'... 'But for too many of our citizens, a different reality exists: Mothers and children trapped in poverty in our inner cities; rusted-out factories scattered like tombstones across the landscape of our nation.'... 'For many decades, we've enriched foreign industry at the expense of American industry.'... ''We've made other countries rich while the wealth, strength, and confidence of our country have disappeared over the horizon. One by one, the factories shuttered and left our shores, with not even a thought about the millions upon millions of American workers left behind. The wealth of our middle class has been ripped from their homes and then redistributed across the entire world.'* In fact, Mrs. Kate Shagall said the same, but used other words and gave a specific examples."

-"No comment!" Mrs. Kate Shagall's response came.

-"I have to add," said my friend the Ambassador, "that I highly appreciate Mrs. Kate Shagall's sincerity. I try to be frank, too. For a career diplomat, to speak sincerely is a proof of courage. Regarding this matter I will tell you a sort of funny story about the differences between a lady and a diplomat. Here it is the funny story. When a lady says no, it means maybe. When she says maybe, she means yes. When she says yes, that means that she is not a lady. No lady, at all. When a diplomat says yes, he means maybe. When he says maybe, he means no. When he says no, means that he is not a diplomat."

All of us, I mean the guests being present in the apartment of my friend the Ambassador, laughed boisterously. The main reason for that heartfelt laugh was the fact that our dinner arrived at the point, where the cognac was served from a bottle on which Emperor Napoleon himself was printed.

Even my colleague Adrian Portzan was cheerful. So he commented: "I think that due to this kind of coniac, in the survey Mr Flora was talking about, the Russians decided that the first foreigner in the top would be Emperor Napoleon. Everybody knows that a lot of drunkards live in Russia. Maybe, for the same reason, their leaders were involving themselves unacceptably in the recent US presidential election with the purpose of making Mrs. Hilary Clinton to lose the last year ballot. That is the reason that, on July 25, 2017, the United States House of Representatives approves *sweeping* sanctions package against Russia. On the TV was said that most of the American newspapers and TV stations, agree with those sanctions. And I know that quite a lot of Americans hate the Russians too."

-"I appreciate the comments of Mr Adrian Portzan." My friend Amy Flora said. "I would like to make some amendments. First, the common Russians don't appreciate cognac; they prefer vodka. Next, I agree with Mr Adrian Portzan that the involvement in other country's presidential election is unacceptable. But, that rule should be applied equally for all countries. A fable of a Romanian writer says: *'I want equality, but not for puppies.'* In the mass-media, they were talking not just about cases of US involvement in the election in different countries... For example, there was much talking about the US involvement in the fall of Salvador Allende, the President of Chile. I know Russians. I graduated my university studies at the Lomonosov University in Moskow."

-"Maybe, that's the reason that you speak so."Adrian Portzan said.

-"Maybe, you're right! Just the same, as far as I know, the Russians admire the Americans and wish to be friends with them. I think that even the actual leaders of Russia wish to have friendly relations with US and with the Americans. So, why intensify the propaganda war?! Why start an economic war?! Qui prodest?! Everything could get out of control and get into a great catastrophe. If step by step, both sides would retaliate, everything could get out of control and get into a great catastrophe."

After a brief silence, I took the floor.

-"I'm sorry, but I want to emphasize what I said before. In November 1970 when I started to work in US for a computer manufacturing Corporation, on the American territory existed the most formidable industry that produced the entire world commodity nomenclature. The American products were most reliable. The productivity, efficiency and inventiveness of Americans were unrivaled in the world. I speak from my experience, as I visited many factories in US, Germany, Japan, France, Austria, China etc. Since then the world has dramatically changed. Part of the American industry moved abroad. *'One by one, the factories shuttered…'* The Americans won the wars (including the cold war). The Germans etc (not to waste your time I will not give the long list of the others) won contracts and customers. They got the markets of certain countries which became in fact colonies of a new type. In those countries, the Germans etc are now the owners of the natural resources, of the natural monopolies and of the most profitable companies. For example, in Bucharest (and in all Romania), almost all luxury cars are Mercedes and BMW. You can not see even one single American Cadillac in this country. A few days ago, in the nearby supermarket, I found only potatoes produced in Germany; though they say that Romania has more fertile soil than

Germany! I think that everything in the quotes I gave from the speech of President Trump represents the real truth. I hope that in the next several years, the USA will succeed in bringing back the industry to the Americans soil. I forgot to mention that Germany managed also to swallow peacefully the so called German Democratic Republic."

-"I think that we should return to the problems facing our country." Professor Badescu said. "It was said here that Romania is a *'de facto'* colony... I see that His Excellency the Ambassador Ionescu is ready to give his opinion."

-"Everything from the definition of colonialism, according to Encyclopædia Britannica, could be found in the situation of nowadays Romania. Its natural resources, are exploited by foreign companies. For example, two important gas resources located in the Romanian territorial waters of the Black Sea were sold to 'Luk Oil' (Russia) and 'OMV' (Austria). According to the signed contracts, our country has the right to receive only 10% of the gas that will be produced; 90% will be exported by the said two companies. The timber from our forests is exported and the furniture is manufactured abroad. The wheat, corn, sunflower, lambs and other raw materials are exported to foreign countries for processing, and the manufactured products are imported to Romania. The existing factories in 1989 were demolished and exported as scrap iron. Thus, Romania became one of the greatest exporter of scrap iron in the world. Over 95% of the bank capital existing in Romania is owned by foreign banks. The insurance companies belong to foreign companies. I could give many other examples. All that was said here makes me conclude that my belief is correct. Romania is a *'de facto'* colony, where citizens have no impact on the course of the country. In Romania, political activities (by vote or street demonstrations) did not and have not any effect on the course of the country and on the population's standard of living. Foreign investments in Romania are highest from Germany, France, Italy, Austria, Belgium etc. Due to low salaries and due to the fact that most of the foreign owned companies in this country transfer their profits before taxation, the profitability of foreign investments in Romania is double compared to that existing in eurozone. To stop the transfer of profits before taxation, in other countries (Hungary etc) the foreign owned companies are overtaxed. Or instead, for the same purpose, the total sales are taxed. In those countries salaries are higher than in Romania."

- "All the same," said Emy Flora, "I would like to tell you that recently, the Romanian government decided to create a Sovereign Investment and Development Fund, as in France, Norway, Saudi Arabia etc. That is very good, I guess, for the Romanians.... Maybe, for that reason, certain political foreign foundations try to block the creation of this Fund; and of rising wages in Romania also. Unfortunately almost everything else is gloomy for the Romanians."

"To listen to your opinions is terrible; you Romanian citizens!" Adrian Portzan said.

Smiling, Emy Flora said: "Let's then hear the opinions of others… *Romania has one of the highest levels of income inequality in European Union, and it is growing,'* is said in a country report released by the European Commission on February 22, 2017. *'Poverty and social exclusion remain high… among the working people is two times higher than the EU average.'* World Vision International, an Evangelical Christian humanitarian organization, reported that *'Romania still lacks adequate social services, including education, health and child protection and the gap between urban and rural poor continues to grow… Disillusioned young people search for a better life abroad -that promise is made to them by businessmen that are actually traffickers. Romania's infant mortality rate is double compared to that of the EU average.'* According to a study carried out by World Vision Romania. *'Almost three quarters of families living in rural areas had difficulties in ensuring their children a quality diet in 2016. Moreover, one in ten children goes to bed hungry.'* In Romania it is an unprecedented demographic decline. The leader of the party that won the legislative **elections** held in Romania on December 11, 2016, declared: *'In 26 years, it was stolen everywhere and were scattered billions of euros... Over 1,300 Romanian factories and workshops have been liquidated, effectively liquidated.'* Not just the wages in the West have caused the mass exodus of the Romanians. A major cause is the fact that millions of jobs (almost half of those existing in 1989) have disappeared. And I could add more..."

-"That's enough!" Adrian Portzan cried out loudly.

-"Just the same," Emy Flora said, "I have to tell you that I am concerned about the economical reasons that are at bottom of today's situation in Romania. Actually, from the value added (or GDP) created in companies whose owners are foreigners, remain in Romania only gross salaries and the contributions for social security, health insurance, unemployment, vacation, accidents and occupational diseases etc. For each employee, all those amount to about 1.25 to 1.30 x gross salary. Wages in this country being from 4 to 9 times lower than in the rich investors countries, means that actually in Romania remains very little. For this reason, even the local politicians began to speak on the TV about the Romanian paradox that is, *'the economy grows' (i e GDP), but 'the standard of living lowers'*. Do you want additional comments?!"

The answer to this question was given by Professor Badescu. "No! That's enough, as our friend Adrian Portzan just said. Let see if the inequality in the world has been amended."

-"No!" Answered my friend the Ambassador. "It went from bad to worse. Eight men own the same wealth as the 3.6 billion people who make up the poorest half of humanity, according to a new report published by Oxfam 16 January 2017. The Executive Director of Oxfam International, said: *'It is obscene for so much wealth to be held in the hands of so few when 1 in 10 people survive on less than $2 a day. Inequality is trapping hundreds of millions in poverty; it is fracturing our societies and undermining democracy'*. I am just reading from the net that the richest 1% people of the world, hold more than the combined wealth owned by the remaining 99% of the world population. Thus, we can see that our world is sick. The richest 1% people of the world are sick in their heart and mind too. They will die as the poorest half population of the planet. They will not take with them their properties to the Heavens. For their greed, they will be sent straight to the Hell."

-"We don't have to forget," said Emy Flora, "that it is wrong the idea promoted by rich countries propaganda that only the progress and the continous development of the rich countries could pull after them the poor countries and determine their development. That way, the gap between the rich and the poor countries will be greater and greater every day. In 1959, C. P. Snow wrote: *'The main issue is that the people in the industrialised countries are getting richer, and those in the non-industrialised countries are at best standing still; so that the gap between the industrialised countries and the rest is widening every day.'* Nowadays is even worse! The rich former European colonial powers *"have helped"* Eastern European countries to get rid of an important part of their industry and economy, and have grabbed their most profitable companies. All this was done with the *"uninterested-help"* and approval of the politicians of Romania, Hungary, Bulgaria, Poland, Czech Republic, Slovakia, Slovenia etc. In the year of 2010 the GDP per capita in the richest country (Qatar) was 263 times higher than the GDP per capita in the poorest country (Congo) in the world. In 2015, i.e. after five years, this ratio (between Luxemburg and Burundi) has increased to 366! That means that the inequality between nations is growing tremendously fast. In case the *'status-quo'* of the world affaires will be maintained, what kind of ratio we will have after other five years?!"

At this point, Emy Flora intervened again.

-"This huge gap between rich and poor countries is the most important reason why the peoples from Africa, Latin America, Middle East, Asia and East Europe started to move toward the rich countries of the West. The wars in Iraq, Syria, Afghanistan, Libya, Sudan etc, represents only the second most important reason. The conclusion that can be drawn from this reality is that the massive exodus toward the rich countries can not be stopped, unless the two causes that I have just mentioned are eliminated. It is unlikely that the current methods by which the rich countries fight against terrorism, will give the expected results. As it has been so far, most immigrants into rich countries will be settled by legal and peaceful means. If the current pace of arrivals from Africa, Asia, the Middle East, Latin America, etc. continues, the demographic structure will change radically in the rich countries. This will happen due to the differences in the natality of ethnic groups and because of the future immigration. I read on the net that in the US, by 2065, the non-

Hispanic whites will be 46% of the overall population (currently 62%). No ethnic group will be a majority. Hispanics will be 24% of the population (18% now), Asians will be 14% (6% now) and blacks will be 13% (12% now). Even more fundamental changes could happen in Great Britain, France, Germany etc. I have to point out that even bigger inequality existed, exists and will exist inside all countries, whether they are rich or poor Nowadays, the former European colonial powers turn to a new economic neocolonialism. Maybe now is the time, for the economic neocolonialism to be also crushed, as in our times, some of the old colonial powers hinder in fact, the development of the other backward countries, even inside the European Union."

At this point of the discussions, my friend the Ambassador wanted to intervene again.

-"You're very right about everything you said! Your ideas about how to improve the situation of poor countries are sensible. Good advice! Oscar Wilde said: *'The only thing to do with good advice is to pass it on. It is never of any use to oneself'* Anyhow, the rich countries will not follow your advice neither. For them, only their interests count. A few days ago I read a book published, in 2001, by a great politician, which is Henry Kissinger. In it he said: *'Companies of developing countries are increasingly being absorbed by American and European multinationals.'* ... *'The fact is that, quite simply, the industrial democracies cannot permit access to Gulf oil to be denied to them or acquiesce in the Gulf's being dominated by a country or group of countries hostile to their well-being.'* Also, he quotes the following statement of President Nixon: *'Our objective, in the first instance, is to support our interests over the long run with a sound foreign policy.'* Who will support really the interests of the poor countries?! Samuel P. Huntington, best known for his 1993 theory, the *'Clash of Civilizations'*, was right when he sustained that this will dominate global politics. Actually, the clash of civilizations has not diminished but intensified more and more every day. During his presidential campaign, Donald Trump said at a October 26, 2016 rally in Charlotte, N.C: *'We've spent $6 trillion on the* wars *in the* Middle East. ... *imagine* **if** *that money had been spent* **at** *home.'*. These all are a proof that wars did not diminish, but have multiplied in our world."

"My lady and gentlemen," said Professor Badescu, "it's time to conclude our discussions. Today I learned a lot. I have to admit that before, I did not know, to a great degree, what you said in these discussions. That is normal! I remember what Shakespeare's Hamlet said to Horatio, i.e.: *'There are more things in heaven and earth, Horatio, than are dreamt of* in *your philosophy*.' That is very true. In today's world occur also more things than I, or anyone else, know of. Maybe, that some of the comments or ideas that we uttered here today are not correct. But, we live in a free country, after all. So, we have the right to make mistakes, too! It is important to think about what is happening to us and to all humankind. Thank you all for your sincerity. Good by!"

July 28, 2017